ELVES

MELISSA
SH

CREATIVE EDUCATION • CREATIVE PAPERBACKS

Published by Creative Education and Creative Paperbacks
P.O. Box 227, Mankato, Minnesota 56002
Creative Education and Creative Paperbacks are imprints of
The Creative Company
www.thecreativecompany.us

Design by The Design Lab
Production by Rachel Klimpel
Art direction by Rita Marshall
Printed in the United States of America

Photographs by Alamy (The Artchives, Picture Lux/The Hollywood
Archive, Pictures Now, V&A Images), Dreamstime (Michael Zech),
Getty Images (Keith Lance/DigitalVision Vectors), iStockphoto
(ZargonDesign), Mary Evans Picture Library (Mary Evans Picture
Library, Medici, The Pictures Now Image Collection), Pixabay
(OpenClipart-Vectors), Shutterstock (HelenaQueen, Atelier Sommer-
land)

Library of Congress Cataloging-in-Publication Data
Names: Gish, Melissa, author.
Title: Elves / Melissa Gish.
Series: Amazing mysteries.
Includes bibliographical references and index.
Summary: A basic exploration of the appearance, behaviors, and
origins of elves, the bad-tempered or helpful magical creatures
known for their tricks or know-how. Also included is a story from
folklore about an elf family that helped a farmer.

Identifiers:
ISBN 978-1-64026-487-8 (hardcover)
ISBN 978-1-68277-038-2 (pbk)
ISBN 978-1-64000-614-0 (eBook)
This title has been submitted for CIP processing under LCCN
2021937336.

First Edition HC 9 8 7 6 5 4 3 2 1
First Edition PBK 9 8 7 6 5 4 3 2 1

Table of Contents

Elves in The Lord of the Rings movies (opposite) are human-sized.

Elves are magical beings. There are two groups. **Domestic** elves live in human homes and on farms. Country elves live in forests, fields, and caves. Some elves are as short as mice. Others are the size of humans.

domestic relating to family life

Wild places such as forests make good hiding places for elves.

The first elves were called *alfar*. Their homeland is Alfheim (*ALV-heym*), according to Norse stories. In Alfheim, there is no sun or moon. It is always **twilight**. Elves still live there.

twilight the period of time before sunrise and after sunset, when the sky glows with soft light

Some elves are said to love music, art, and nature.

Norway's Vikings took elf **folklore** to Iceland about 1,000 years ago. Icelandic people called elves *huldufólk.* This name means "hidden people."

folklore traditional beliefs, stories, or customs that are passed on by word of mouth

Some elves are not nice. The tiny ellefolk of Denmark raise cows that are blue. Humans' cows that wander onto ellefolks' land get sick. German elves sit on a sleeper's chest and cause bad dreams.

The blue cows of ellefolk live on dew rather than grass or other food.

Most elves are kind. The elves of Uganda are called emandwa. Their magic protects mothers and babies. In Scotland, elves watch over babies so bad fairies do not steal them.

In some stories from around the world, elves live among flowers.

In Quebec and Ontario, elves sleep through the winter. In spring, the Elf Queen spreads warmth to melt the snow. Then the elves awaken.

An elf queen uses her powers to protect others.

Mushrooms are often tied to magical creatures, from elves and gnomes to fairies.

Country elves love to snack on mushrooms. In Wales, elves are called ellyllon. They eat fairy butter. This is a **fungus** that grows in the rotting roots of old trees.

fungus a living thing like a mushroom or mold that feeds on dead or living things

In a poem written in 1823, Santa Claus is an elf who lives at the North Pole. Later, stories of Santa's elves were told. They build toys in his workshop.

The 1823 poem is known by many titles, including "'Twas the Night Before Christmas."

Today, elves are protected by law in Iceland. Builders must not disturb elves. Roads must curve around rocks and hills where elves are thought to live.

Tiny elf houses in Iceland warn people that elves might be in the area.

An Elf Story

A family of elves made their home on a farm. They built a tiny house under the roots of an old tree. They used their magic to help the farmer. They fed horses and milked cows. They raked hay and picked corn. All they asked in return was to be left alone. But the farmer was curious. One day while the elves worked, he peeked inside their home. The elves left and never returned.

Read More

Knudsen, Shannon. *Fairies and Elves*. Minneapolis: Lerner, 2010.

Lawrence, Sandra. *The Atlas of Monsters*. Philadelphia: Running Press Kids, 2019.

Shutter, Aaron. *A Field Guide to Elves, Dwarves, and Other Magical Folk*. Mankato, Minn.: Capstone, 2015.

Websites

Kiddle: Elf Facts for Kids
https://kids.kiddle.co/Elf
Read about elves in history.

Santasnorthpole: Fun Stuff for Kids
https://www.santasnorthpole.com
Find facts, games, and activities about Christmas elves.

Note: Every effort has been made to ensure that the websites listed above are suitable for children, that they have educational value, and that they contain no inappropriate material. However, because of the nature of the Internet, it is impossible to guarantee that these sites will remain active indefinitely or that their contents will not be altered.

Index